The Person Within You

Destroying the Power of the Terrorist Recruiter

by
Justice The Salute

Proudly Published in the USA by

Justice the Salute
c/o BTBI
17011 Lincoln Ave #408
Parker, CO 80134

ISBN: 1530839483

Dedication

I give thanks to my divine maker, my wife, my family, my friends and the brave men and women who gave their lives fighting terrorism while serving in the United States Armed Forces.

I salute the men and women around the world who are fighting terrorism today. I am dedicated to fighting terrorism around the world. We can win the fight against terrorism around the world through the cooperation of countries in the international community around the world.

I cannot stress how important it is to fight terrorism in the world today. It threatens our gift to us by our Maker as a human being to be free to choose their own religious belief, their own agenda and a life when it comes to their lifestyle; to choose the method they worship their Maker or if they do not, to choose to worship any religion, or any sect.

I strongly believe that women around the world should not be abused in any way, shape, form or fashion. I believe that women should not be abused

4

sexually or mistreated because of their sex or their religious belief. I believe that women should have the rights that every other human being in the world enjoys as long as it does not interfere with the rights of other people.

As a writer of the person within me, I am formally dedicated to the principles that are stated in the book The Person Within You.

Table of Contents

Part II

Introduction

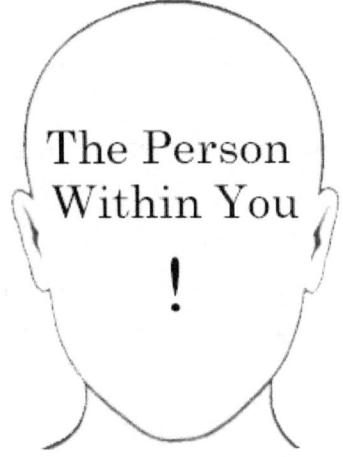

The Person
Within You
!

Never in the history of the world has there been ruthlessness or mass murder carried out by ISIS and other terrorist groups as it is today.

Terrorist groups have been able to obtain large amounts of material assets to support their terrorist threats in killing innocent people around the world. Some terrorist groups have been able to obtain supplies and support from some countries around the world.

A country that supports terrorism should be identified and isolated. These countries should be charged with war crimes against humanity. It is a grave concern that somehow a terrorist group may be able to obtain a weapon of mass destruction, and that they would not hesitate to use it to kill large numbers of innocent people. If fighting terrorism is to be successful in Syria, Iraq and all countries in the Middle East, countries around the world must become involved in the fight against terrorism. Terrorism is not just a threat to a few countries in the world. Terrorism is a threat to all countries in the international community and its people. As you read the book, can you answer this question? Is the world safer from terrorism today than it was 10 years ago? Have hate groups interrupted your lives in any way?

No one should be killed because of his or her race, or their agenda, their religious belief, their sex, or their love for humanity, because the terrorists desire to control his life's agenda. This should not happen because one does not believe in the agenda of a terrorist organization.

Part I

Chapter 1

Destroying the Power of the Terrorist Recruiter

The problem with terrorist groups today, like ISIS and other terrorist organizations, is that years ago they did not have the capabilities to spread terrorism as they do today. This causes a great danger to the world and all peaceful nations around the world. Terrorist groups today have managed to infiltrate countries in the Middle East, specifically Syria and Iraq. One of the problems is that they are creating large numbers of refugees who flee their country because they do not feel safe there. Countries that have divisions in their political system, cause a breeding place for terrorist organizations such as ISIS. Terrorist groups have been around for a long time but only their message of spreading terrorism has changed. They have moved into the scientific arena using technology to destroy and spread threats to the world and to kill innocent people if they do not conform to their agenda.

Terrorist groups not only are a threat to all countries but terrorist groups that have permeated America have killed numerous people for example September 11, 2001. The current day political division in governments throughout the world and corruption, have made it easy for terrorist group leaders to assign their organizations to the groups in these countries for example, in the Middle East. Extremist and their groups all have one thing in common. They will destroy artifacts and the cultural items in museums and other religious places in the country in which they are in.

Women, children and older people in a country where terrorism is active and occupying a portion of a country, will be killed because they do not assimilate with the agenda of the terrorist organization. Groups such as ISIS and other terrorist groups, will associate themselves with Islamic Muslim groups. They may associate with Christian groups in some way or another and claim that they are a real representative of the organization, but they are not. Hate groups and terrorist groups have adopted a system in which they will hide their faces and even their fighting forces.

One of the problems with modern terrorist groups' is that they are allowed to go in and out of some countries very easily and their operations are not protected. America and other countries in the world are subject to the terrorists and their threats. Terrorist groups will follow their leader's instructions whatever it may be. They inform their followers to engage in field campaigns. This is done by using communications of their targets and have it displayed in the news media throughout the world which are scare tactics. Never before in the history of terrorism have they displayed beheadings through the news media, until now.

The terrorist group leaders will train their recruiters in the modern science of recruiting. The recruiter uses modern methods of recruiting . The terrorist recruiter has a major role in the functions of the terrorist group organization. The recruiter is one of the main ways of obtaining manpower for the terrorist group. The more men and women a terrorist group recruiter can recruit, the more dangerous that group will become to the world. This will cause more innocent lives to be lost around the world. What is so frightening is the large number of men and women the recruiter has been able to recruit from countries around the world by use of the world wide web. It is well known that a terrorist group recruiter will associate themselves with another hate group in countries throughout the world. In some cases, the terrorist group recruiter will find it easy to recruit members of a hate group.

Terrorist group recruiters will not only recruit candidates for the organization for the manpower to fight against and kill innocent people in the world, they also will recruit other terrorist groups in the country they are occupying. This comes under the category of homegrown terrorist recruiting. Terrorist group recruiters will take advantage of young men and women because of their lack of knowledge of worldly events and terrorist activities. A terrorist group recruiter has been trained to know potential candidates by the vibes that they give him. A terrorist group recruiter will welcome a former military person because they will bring valuable military knowledge to their organization.

Often times a terrorist recruiter will take advantage of a civilian who does not understand why they are being recruited by a terrorist group. The more men and women a terrorist group recruiter can recruit, the more innocent lives will be lost. Extremist group recruiters may use the elements of trust to develop a feeling of acceptance between you and him. One will feel that he has your best interest at heart as well as his own. Extremist group recruiters are the main cause of bloodshed in Syria and Iraq and other countries in the Middle East. ISIS is an organization that has had great success with their recruiting around the world including the United States.

These are some of the main means extremist groups may use to recruit people around the world. One may be by word of mouth, by cell phone, by the internet and the use of other communication devices. What may be hard to understand is why so many people will let an extremist group recruit them to kill innocent people. We are vulnerable to extremist group recruiters because we have not been educated in terrorist groups recruiting activities. In the pre 911 era, we have never had to deal with the level of terrorism we have today.

We are very social in America. The terrorist group recruiter will take advantage of this and our social habits to recruit people for their organization.

In America some of us will invite others into their home without knowing his or her background. A person who has a financial problem may become a victim of an extremist group recruiter because of the promises the recruiter will give them help to eliminate their financial problem, and the one recruited may become a member of an extremist organization because of this.

In America we have people coming in and out of our country intentionally from all around the world. This is a danger to our national security. This makes it easy for a terrorist group recruiter to recruit, in some cases without being detected. We must remember that terrorist groups can be your next door neighbor, they can be a citizen of the United States or they can be a person that comes from another country who supports terrorist organizations.

To destroy the activities of a terrorist group organization recruiter, we must eliminate his source from which his finances derive. It is a possibility that some of his finances may come from sympathizers or supporters who have been associated with his organization. This is why we must be trained to understand what terrorism really is and how dangerous they are to America and the international community. Countries internationally must join forces to destroy terrorism and their recruiters. Fighting terrorist group recruiters by eliminating group communication and functions with other terrorist recruiters, will save innocent lives. All countries in the world have a duty to destroy terrorist recruiters. If countries can destroy the ability of terrorist recruiters to recruit new members, it will save thousands of lives in the world including America.

When a terrorist group recruiter is captured, they should be tried in a court of law for wartime crimes against humanity. A terrorist group recruiter's aim is not just destroying the innocent; it is to destroy culture, religious belief, freedom as a human being, freedom to choose his way of life, and freedom to worship in the manner that one desires. This is how the person within you comes into being. The person within you has the freedom to worship your religious belief which was given to you by your Divine Maker. The person within you gave you the life to teach, to live, to enjoy and to share with your family and friends. Also, with other people that believe in human rights and the dignity of humanity.

Terrorist groups, such as ISIS, fighting in Syria and Iraq are destroying family structure, killing innocent people and destroying artifacts. Teachers and other important people of culture and historical artifacts that have been passed down through the centuries up until today, are destroyed in one act of terrorism. This is why we must stop the terrorist groups from recruiting.

The terrorist group recruiter will not reveal to his candidates his agenda. He will not tell you that you may be recruited to be a suicide bomber. One may be used for sexual pleasure in some manner, if one is female.

Women are very vulnerable to terrorist group recruiters because they will make promises to them. Young women are good candidates because they may have fantasies about the pleasures of life that a terrorist group may promise. A terrorist group recruiter will not initially tell them that they must comply to their agenda, if not, they will be killed. They will not tell them that once they become a member of the terrorist group organization, they will not be able to leave that organization.

In conclusion, we must not grow weary in the face of ISIS and their recruiters and other terrorist group recruiters because innocent people's lives are at stake. The press of darkness is on the move and all nations of the world must come together against ISIS and other terrorist group recruiters. We must stop terrorist killing of Muslims, Christians and Jewish people around the Middle East. We must not forget that we have had the flow of terrorism in

America. We will not let terrorist groups around the world destroy us and our culture. In our hearts and mind, we as a people of religion, freedom and belief, must not allow terrorist groups and hate groups and any other group that aims to destroy humanity, take our freedoms from us in America.

No matter how grave the situation may seem when it comes to the destruction of ISIS and any other terrorist group, we as Americans and other peace-loving countries can overcome terrorism by uniting and fighting with all that is necessary to defeat the terrorist groups that are operating the world today.

There is hope. We must have the will to fight terrorism with all resources available to us. Together with other free nations that have the love for humanity, we can stop the killing of innocent people around the world.

Chapter 2

Destroying the Power of the Recruiter with Education

America and the international community are in danger of innocent people being killed because of the terrorist group recruiters. This is why it is very important that education about extremist recruiters should be taught at a very early stage to all people. We must teach our children at an early age that terrorist groups and extremist groups are opportunists. Their main agenda is to spread terrorism and to recruit members to increase their terrorist group organization activities. In the United States, the recruiter may be your next door neighbor or he may be a person from another country. He will not let you know his true agenda. Families in neighborhoods around our country should educate their citizens about terrorism organizations operating in their community. We should teach in our schools, our churches and in our neighborhood meetings, about ISIS. We can educate people about how they recruit. We must teach our children that terrorist groups will make false promises to get people into their organization. They will not tell you the facts about their organization and their agenda. We must show our children examples of someone who would approach them who could be identified as an extremist recruiter because they do not have knowledge of their agenda.

We must learn about recruiters and their methods of acquiring people. We must be able to assess the situation mentally and have the ability to know if they are approached by a terrorist group recruiter. They must have to ask for time to think about their offer before joining the organization.

All schools and colleges throughout the world should have a terrorist group training course about the danger of the terrorists group recruiting. One way to destroy the terrorist group recruiter is to form neighborhood watch committees in all communities all across the country and in all countries. The neighborhood watch committee should be a part of the law enforcement agency in that area and a big part of the judicial system in countries around the world. Every country should have an element of training in their community about the terrorist group recruiter.

We must have literary equipment and books and information about terrorism and their recruiters. The history of terrorism should be accessible to all people. They should have the use of video surveillance and other devices that detect the operations of terrorist group organizations. Educating people in your community and around the world about the characteristics of terrorist recruiters will save thousands of lives in Iraq and Syria and in the United States.

Each country should have a place in their law enforcement agencies for swift punishment for terrorist group recruiters. This is why it is extremely important that we as a country should be well trained to detect terrorist group organizations operations. Religious groups and all organizations affiliated with churches should have training sessions about how to detect a terrorist group recruiter in order to detect if someone is operating in your neighborhood. We as an international community should teach about the history of terrorism and how it started. The more knowledge that people in your community have about how terrorist recruiters use tactics and terrorism recruiting, the safer it will be for everyone.

Terrorist groups are well educated in the manner in which they may recruit a candidate. Terrorist groups will use groups that have hate and dislike for one another and recruit them into their organization. The knowledge that people have about the terrorist group recruiter and how he is a threat to all human beings in the world today. Its important we must not allow a terrorist group to know our agenda when it comes to recognizing his operation within a neighborhood.

The recruiter will usually operate in an area in which people have no knowledge of him or about the organization with which he is recruiting from.

Recognizing a terrorist group recruiter is the most important thing for you and your safety and the safety of others. He will recruit you by not letting you know what lies ahead until after you become a member of his organization.

One reason you must educate yourself about terrorism is because you do not know how they plan to use you in their operation. If you are not aware of the agenda of the terrorist group recruiter, they could promise you a promise they do not plan to keep, and you may be a person for any use in their organization. We have to destroy the recruiter's power through the use of pictures and world events. We must use the information that comes through our local law enforcement agencies and through the investigation of yourself. We have to be watchful for activities that seem unusual in your neighborhood and to recognize activities and crime because remember the duty of the recruit organization is to not let you know their agenda until you became a member of their organization. Terrorist groups use propaganda to lure people into their group. If a person knows the true extent of the terrorist group recruiter, he would not join because of the education that they had received about them.

Education is the most powerful tool that can be used against terrorist group organizations and their recruits . If you have the proper training to detect their operations and their agendas, it would be safer for you and people around you. When you as a citizen educate yourself, your children, people in your churches, people in your synagogues and people in places where information of terrorist groups may be, you could save lives. The terrorist group recruiter that recruits from your country may be a person that could be destroying lives in Syria and Iraq and parts of the Middle East.

To destroy terrorist group actions, you have to stop their ability to recruit in your neighborhood and the men and women who may be potential candidates for the terrorist group organization will save their lives by having knowledge about the terrorist group agenda. The terrorist group recruiter will not tell you that you may be used as a suicide bomber or used to kill a mother, older person or anyone that does not agree with the organization's agenda.

We must remember that terrorists in the world today are in the same scientific arena as we are when it comes to technology. Terrorist group organizations may recruit finances from a person that is capable of giving aid to them. This is why a terrorist group recruit doesn't recruit just for personnel but may recruit for finances for his organization. Not only is his recruiting for personnel important, it is also important for the functions of his organization in a financial manner.

A terrorist group recruiter may recruit you for a recruiting job in another country or in the United States. Terrorist group recruiters may use a citizen of a country for the purpose of recruiting you as a citizen or a person from another country.

A terrorist may be discovered by a citizen or a law enforcement officer who may have the knowledge of how terrorist group recruiters may by operating in your community. Training about a recruiter and his ways of recruiting in your neighborhood, may save people's lives if they have the knowledge of the recruiter group's agenda. To destroy the power of a terrorist group recruiter, you must have education and knowledge of that group's agenda and of his ways of disguising his true goals and agendas.

By repelling and destroying the terrorist group members recruiters, it will save your life and many lives around the world. Teaching and educating people about the tactics of terrorist group operators and how they can deceive you in their statements and their promises, can save lives around the world. Remember all terrorist group recruiters have one thing in common; they will not reveal their true agenda or true organization until you become a member of their organization.

This is why it is very important that we must destroy the ability of the terrorist group recruiter. It will save lives in Syria, in Iraq, in America and in all countries. All humanitarians should teach and train their organizations about the danger of terrorist recruiters and how they can save lives in their country. I cannot stress how important it is for the whole country and every conscious community to train themselves about the danger of terrorist group recruiters. With the destruction of the power of the terrorist group recruiters it is a safety factor for every person in every country, including America. We must not forget 911.

Chapter 3

Destroying The Power Of The Terrorist Group Recruiter Through Psychology

The extremist group will use the power of suggestion to influence a person into a terrorist group organization. This is how "The Person Within You" will come into action and will give you information about what you may be recruited into. This is where you should make a mental assessment of the situation. You should never join an organization that you are not familiar with or an organization in which you have not assessed their agenda.

When you as a person are approached by a recruiter of any kind, you must examine the offer that he/she is offering you. This means making a mental assessment of that offer. You must think about how his gesture to the offer will affect you in a personal manner. You must think about the things that the recruiter may promise you.

You must also rely on your personal knowledge about the situation in which the recruiter is inviting you in to. You must tell the recruiter that you would like to have more time to study the offer in which he is inviting you.

You must assess in your own memory of how it will affect your personal life, your religious belief and of what value is it for you to join the organization. How will the joining of the organization affect your family, the lives of others, and the real aspects of the recruiting offer to you? Does the organization respect the rights of women? How will the recruiter explain to you how you will be affected in your social life?

The recruiter will not tell you about the mistreatment or sexual abuse of women when you join their organization. Terrorist recruiters have been trained to use mind games to play on the knowledge that you do not know or do not understand.

When a terrorist group recruiter recruits you, their aim is to deceive. They will not let you know that their organization does not allow you to control your own life.

The terrorist group recruiter will not let you know that his organization has plans to control you.

Terrorist group recruiters will not tell you that you may be used in any manner in which the terrorist group may have need for, when you are recruited into their organization.When terrorist groups recruit people, they will not tell you that you will lose your freedom of speech and expression. You will only learn this when you become a member.

The organization of terrorist recruiters may happen in your neighborhood or by a person from a foreign country. This comes into the area of homegrown terrorism.

A recruiter may recruit you because you may have a special knowledge or trained in a special field of education or science or have information that will be of great value to the organization.

A recruiter will recruit you into his organization without telling you his agenda disregarding race, culture, religious belief and the will to live your life as you see fit as long as it doesn't interfere in the lives of others.

The terrorist group recruit will not reveal his/her true identity to you because he/she has been indoctrinated through their organization to deceive you until you become a member. Then, you will know the true identity of who they really are. This is the most dangerous factor when you are recruited into a terrorist organization. You will no longer be able to control your life, your desires or your agenda for your lifestyle and your religious belief.

Terrorist groups will find it easy to recruit hate group members because they all have the same thing in common, hate and the destruction of innocent people. A terrorist group recruiter will not reveal to you that his organization is a hate group unless he has received vibes from you that you believe in his agenda. That agenda is, killing innocent people and destroying their families, their synagogues, their churches and their historic artifacts.

When you eliminate the terrorist group recruiter, you are destroying his recruiting message to eliminate people. Their message is to use fear because his organization uses it to make the threat of terrorism their agenda. A terrorist group recruiter is the direct source of power through personnel in which the organization operates.

A terrorist group recruiter recruits you, with the intent of deceiving you. He will not tell you that his organization has plans to take away your ability to control your own thoughts and mental abilities. He will not tell you that when you join his organization, your self esteem will be taken away from you and you will become controlled by the terrorist group organization.The terrorist organization recruiter has been trained psychologically to conceal the terrorist groups plan because if you have knowledge of it, he could not recruit you.

The terrorist group recruiter's goal is to recruit as many vulnerable men and women as possible.

The recruiter will not tell you that his organization is engaged in death, destruction and threats to people, especially people who live in the Middle East. Terrorist group recruiters will not tell you that you may be a part of their psychological plan.

People in all communities around the globe must be trained psychologically to know when they are being used by the power of suggestion by a terrorist group recruiter.

Chapter 4

Destroying The Power Of The Terrorist Group Recruiter Through Technology

We can track the terrorist group recruiters through special technology such as surveillance cameras and cell phones. We can track terrorist group recruiters through travel agencies by tracking devices on buses and using body cameras.

With special electronic devices, we may be able to detect a terrorist group recruiter at the time he is trying to recruit someone. Banks, hospitals, businesses, city parks and other areas where a terrorist group could recruit a candidate, can be detected by special equipment. When large sums of money are sent to other countries by unknown groups or other organizations, the terrorist activity may be detected by electronic technology. We can fight terrorist group recruiters through international law enforcement in countries around the world with mobile technology. Technology has also made it possible to detect terrorist groups through the use of DNA forensic evidence.

When terrorist groups travel, their movements can be detected in ports of entry around the world. This makes it easy for countries that are fighting terrorism to keep track of a terrorist recruiter's activities through international communication. A terrorist group recruiter may use electronic technology which makes it vulnerable to detect the technology and his operation. This is why international law enforcement agencies and organizations that are fighting terrorism can detect a terrorist group operator by monitoring their activities. Terrorist group recruiters may use some known technology but he must use this technology in a manner that will not be detected.

Cell phones are good devices that can detect a terrorist group operation without that group detecting it. A terrorist group recruiter may be detected by a listening device that may be attached to a person that he may be planning to recruit as a candidate for his organization.

The internet can be a good tool to check the activities of a terrorist group recruiter.

Some terrorist group recruiters may use electronic code in communicating with their organization. This is why we must have technology to decode a terrorist group's communication system. A terrorist group recruiter will sometimes use electronic devices to recruit a candidate for his/her organization. The drone is a good way to detect a terrorist group recruiter with an electronic device that an extremist may be carrying aboard any mode of transportation. A satellite device may be used in a special manner to detect a recruiter's operation in an area where he does not expect it to be detected.

A ring or a button on an individual can be used to detect the operation of a terrorist group recruiter in your area, in areas around the country and in other countries.

The use of modern day technology is a great tool to use in detecting and destroying the terrorist group recruiter in areas around the world. Animals can also be used as a tool in tracking or revealing an operation of a terrorist group recruiter in neighborhoods around the country.

The technology that we have today that we use to detect a terrorist group recruiter, will save lives in our country and countries around the world.

As time changes, so has the technology we have used to detect the terrorist group recruiter's operations in various areas. The United States and its allies and countries around the world must use the latest technology in detecting terrorist group recruiters that may be operating in their country.

Through the use of the technology that we have today, if used properly, we can defeat the terrorist group organization recruiter and save thousands of innocent lives around the world. We must use the latest technology that we have at our disposal in fighting ISIS and other terrorist groups around the world.

As scientific methods of detecting terrorist group recruiters improve, we must instill these methods into our new system of detecting terrorist group recruiters and their organization

With the latest scientific methods of fighting terrorist group recruiters and destroying their recruiting ability, will save lives not only in Syria, Iraq but in other countries, including the United States. We must not grow weary in the fight against terrorist group recruiting because with the will to win we will win and put a stop to the terrorist group threats and the killing of innocent people.

With the coming together of all countries through out the world that have the love of humanity to fight terrorism, whatever organization it may be, will save the lives of innocent people in their country. This will defeat ISIS and other terrorist groups and cause governments to be able to control their own country's activities without the invasion of terrorists and hate groups.

Chapter 5

A Call to Action Against Terrorism and Their Recruiters

Reasons and ways to get involved:

Legislature to call for information about fighting terrorism within your community.

Contact Your:

- Police Department
- Your Neighborhood Judicial Department
- Your Citizen Advocacy Group
- The Federal Bureau of Investigation
- Your Citizen Hot Line
- Homeland Security Agency
- Your City Security Division

State Legislator:

You may contact your state legislator about forming a terrorist watch group committee in your neighborhood.

When a terrorist group watch committee is formed in a neighborhood, your local law enforcement agency should be a part of the function of your committee.

Call to Action Against Terrorism and Their Recruiters:

Ways to get involved. Provide financial support for refugees in countries that have been invaded by terrorist groups such as ISIS:

- Write to your state representative to call for aid relief for refugees around the world.
- Provide financial support to World Vision, a Christian organization that is helping Syrian and Iraq refugees in the crisis in that area.

As a family member and a humanitarian, we must think about actions we can take to protect ourselves against terrorism. We must think about the protection of our future from terrorist activities. We must learn that our protection comes from the cooperation of countries that are willing to fight terrorism with us and support our cause for the saving of innocent lives in Iraq, Syria and other nations. This starts in our cities, our neighborhoods and all around the world. The lives that we save in other countries will enable the world to be a better place to live. We must defend our religious belief and our political beliefs of freedom to express our right to vote and choose our leaders. We must fight terrorism at all levels with all means at our disposal.

We must search for knowledge and understanding on how to defeat the ability of terrorist groups such as ISIS. To win you must have the will to win. If you have the will to win you can defeat the enemy. Nothing is impossible.

Together as a world community we can and will defeat groups like ISIS and other terrorist groups.

To defeat a terrorist group such as ISIS, we must use psychology. We must use technology. We must use military power. We must use military science. We must use communication and we must use the will of the people around the world to join in the fight against terrorism.

The larger the force against a terrorist group such as ISIS, the better the chances are in defeating this organization. This call for action should be directed to all the governing officials around the world. Army, Navy and Air Force should be involved in the fight against terrorism in Syria and Iraq. Stopping the spread of terrorism in the Middle East could be a key to stopping threats to America. The fight against terrorism may seem like there are just a few countries involved, but terrorism can be a threat to all free nations around the world.

Unless we all get involved in fighting terrorism, it will spread into the country that you are living in. If we stop terrorism in the world today, it will make it safer for all human beings around the world in their neighborhoods, in their villages, in their municipalities and in their governments. This will bring an end to migration as a result of war because of the terrorist activities and the people not feeling safe to live in their own country.

For the safety of all the world, we must stop terrorism wherever it may occur before it spreads to a point of no control. It's in the Middle East now, but it's very likely that it can spread to all parts of the world.

Remember 911.

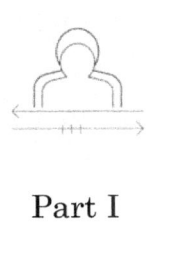

Part I

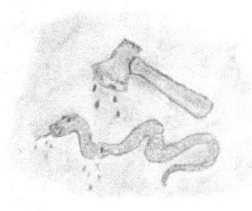

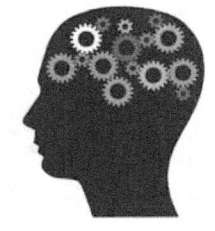

Conclusion

It is well known that ISIS and all terrorist groups around the world are carrying out destruction and other death threats along with the killing of innocent people. They do it because people do not agree with their murderous agenda. The terrorist group recruiters are one of the main means of the groups' power to kill innocent people and destroy cultural artifacts in Syria and Iraq. To stop the terrorist group recruiter we must destroy his power. This is essential to the safety of all people around the world and in the Middle East.

The terrorist recruiter is the main source of manpower, which is essential to the ISIS organization. Terrorist group operations in the United States, are one of the main elements in which terrorist group recruiters use to entice young men and women in the United States. To stop this activity, we must use the power of education, the power of psychology, and the power of technology.

Terrorist recruiters' power to recruit must be destroyed through education not only in the United States but countries around the world. The power of psychology is one method that must be used to destroy the power of the terrorist recruiter. When the recruiter uses the power of suggestion to influence young men and women that are not aware of his agenda, they will join the terrorist group organization because they do not have the knowledge of the terrorist group's hidden agenda.

Destroying the power of the terrorist group recruiter through technology can be a valuable asset for the safety of innocent people's lives in Syria, Iraq and abroad. Civilian cameras, cell phones, hand-held devices and internet, and other listening devices and other means of telecommunication, will play a great part in destroying the power of a recruiter in your neighborhoods and communities.

Countries must communicate in the use of the power to destroy the terrorist recruiters in their countries. This will make it safe in the countries in which the terrorist group recruiter is recruiting and make it safer for all people. The terrorist group recruiter has been known to recruit young men and women through the internet with smart phones.

Destroying the power to recruit through these avenues will detour operations in your neighborhood and neighborhoods around the world. Countries must join the fight against terrorist group recruiters through the use of satellite surveillance. To interrupt the communications between a terrorist group recruiter and its organization's leader is essential in saving of lives, avoiding destruction of property, of cultural artifacts and of people's religious beliefs around the world.

The Person within you will give you the encouragement and knowledge to know when you are being recruited by a terrorist group recruiter. We as human beings were given certain powers to control our thoughts and our behaviors when it comes to observing organizations that you know nothing about and what their agenda may be. "The Person With in You" is the inherited right that your

Divine Maker gave you through your creation, known as the will to choose what's good for you as a human being.

A terrorist group recruiter can easily recruit someone with mental illness of some kind because they are not able to easily assess what is good for them. However, a person with a sound mind can reason what's good or safe for him when the terrorist group recruiter approaches him with terrorist group recruiting tactics. A recruiter will observe a candidate for his organization by the vibes he receives from him regarding his financial affairs.

This is why people with financial difficulties should do research before they accept an offer in a financial manner from anyone prior to joining the organization, especially a terrorist group.

Destroying the power of the terrorist group through education, psychology and technology will save lives in Syria, in Iraq and in the Middle East. It will help eliminate the growing problem of the refugee camps and the migration pattern throughout the world because of the terrorist groups harmful activity.

This is not only a threat to other countries around the world; it is a threat to America and people.

Part II

Chapter 6

The Fight Against
Terrorism

"The Person Within You" informs you on how to observe the terrorist groups that are destroying property, destroying lives of people in Syria and in Iraq. You must imagine how it would be if your country was a victim of the terrorism that is occurring in Syria and in Iraq and in the Middle East. You must think of what you can do to help the victims of terrorism.

There are many things that people can do to fight against terrorism. One is to strengthen whatever belief you have and make your religious and cultural beliefs stronger. You can do this by supporting the men and women that are fighting in various ways to stop the growth of terrorism.

Terrorist operations are started by people who will engage in supporting extremism and violence. They will associate with people who may be engaged in corruption in a government that terrorist groups operate in. It is the duty of all people that have the love of humanity in their hearts to report people who are engaged in terrorist groups. They must report people who are engaged in hate groups in a neighborhood and in a country in which they live. The sources to report suspected people who are engaged in terrorism in the U.S. are Homeland Security, the US military arm and the political representative in your country and in your state government.

People will flee their countries when they feel it is not safe to live there anymore. ISIS and other terrorist groups in Syria, Iraq and around the world are one of the main causes of refugee camps and migrations from countries in the Middle East.

If terrorist groups do not destroy you in your home town now, they will disrupt your way of life, and your social life. They will disrupt your religious beliefs and try to destroy your synagogues, your churches and your agenda for your family lifestyle. This is what terrorism is about. It is about destruction and the killing of innocent people anywhere possible.

I'm sure that when some of you read the book "The Person Within You," you will think of what you can do to fight against terrorism in your country with whatever means are at your disposal. For example, a child may set up a lemonade stand and give the proceeds to an organization that is supporting refugee camps. That means that you don't have to give millions of dollars.

The problem today, when it comes to fighting terrorism, is that some countries will use the terrorist group situation for the division of a country during civil war for their own advantage. The countries should come together and curtail the operation of nations who engage in such operations. This can be done through the United Nations.

The dangers of terrorism must never be forgotten because the same terrorists and other groups are planning to continue spreading terrorism not only in countries away from America but in America. They plan to create death and destruction. We must never forget 911 and the homegrown terrorism in Oklahoma and how it destroyed lives in our own country. We must remember 9/12/2001, the day when everyone came together in love and support for one another. It is so unfortunate for men, women, children and all people that have been killed because of their gender or religious beliefs . Every living person should have the right to live in their home without the fear of terrorism and the threat of death to their family and to their neighborhood and to the country in which they live.

When terrorism is embedded in a country that cannot defend itself or its citizens, the women, children, the old and sick people are the ones affected the most.

To kill entire villages because the people in the village are suspected of not complying with the terrorist group's agenda is one of the greatest atrocities that could happen to any living being.

Terrorist groups today have advanced their tactics of destruction while killing innocent people, especially in the Middle East. Terrorist group leaders have advanced in military technology and have used it against armies of different nations. This makes it difficult for some countries' to fight against terrorism when they do not have the will to fight. They must not give up because there is always hope in the fight against terrorism.

America is not perfect. We have gangs and hate groups in our country, but we as Americans manage to live and fight against these groups without getting the entire country involved. Our military and law enforcement agencies have been able to control the actions of hate groups and terrorist planning groups in the United States. We must give credit to the military and the law enforcement agencies in our country.

We cannot forget that America is strong. America holds freedom and hope for all its citizens. America is the greatest country in the world when it comes to humanitarian actions when it comes together, when a tragedy occurs, whatever it may be, America is strong. Some citizens may stray away from the principles of our heritage but this is not the action of the true American citizens.

In the Middle East, countries such as Syria and Iraq are a few of the most dangerous countries in the world. This a threat to our national security throughout the world.

One of the ways that terrorism has impacted society, is by denying people who love to travel and enjoy cultures and ways of life in other countries, the opportunity to visit these places. Terrorist groups such as the Islamic State are destroying these freedoms and treasures.

Terrorist groups have been able to spread their acts of terrorism through the use of communications such as internet and other avenues in which they may be able to spread their fears to the world. We must curtail the actions of terrorist groups who receive arms, supplies and financial backing from supporting countries. These countries should be held accountable for their actions because they create a direct line to the killing of innocent people from all walks of life.

I do believe that terrorist groups such as ISIS will be defeated because the world can no longer tolerate the killing, destruction and damage that they are creating today. People must not grow weary in the face of terrorism and the fight against terrorist groups such as the Islamic State.

The people of the world must come together for the safety of their own country and for the safety of countries throughout the international community to destroy the agendas of terrorist groups that seek to destroy the lives of other people simply because of their own agenda.

The fight against terrorism in the world will not only save lives in countries occupied by terrorists, but will save our own American citizens. This will be a result of the actions we take against terrorism today.

Chapter 7

Fighting Terrorism with the Power of World Coalition

Terrorist group leaders have put together strategies in science to fight with armies that are embedded in a country. This is why countries that are fighting terrorism should receive help from coalition groups. Countries that are fighting terrorism should be fighting the terrorist group for a true cause, not for the cause of their own agenda. Terrorist groups can be defeated if countries come together and fight for a true agenda which is to save lives and stop the terrorists destruction of countries they are embedded in.

The world must find means and ways to eliminate terrorism in Syria and countries in that region and internationally. If the fight against terrorism in Syria and Iraq fails in the Middle East, it will spread to other countries including America.

Coalition groups, when fighting terrorism, must use air power, naval power and military troops on the ground. This is essential because there are many key operations that can be destroyed by ground troops denial of the enemy's access to their supplies, and by their movements.

Coalition groups, when fighting terrorist groups in Syria and Iraq, must use modern science in military weaponry and tactics. They must incorporate strategies that never have been used before in military action. Military powers must come together at the U.N. and assess the actions that terrorist groups are engaged in. They must come to conclusions of what should be done to curtail the terroristic destruction, murder and threats and what should be done to stop their actions.

When a country harbors and aids terrorist groups they should be held accountable for it because they are becoming a part of an organization's operations. All accounting should be done through the international community which prosecutes people who engage in killing and try them as war criminals.

The power of a coalition can be a great deterrent in the destruction of a terrorist group operation. The world community can eliminate terrorist groups by the number of groups that join the world coalition against terrorism. The greater the number of countries that participate and fight against terrorism, the greater the chances of victory there will be. This will save lives of coalition members and innocent people around the globe.

Coalition groups which are well trained and work together are a great asset to the victory that must be achieved when fighting against terrorist groups.

Coalition groups can share their military strategies and their military munitions

Terrorism in the Middle East must be stopped by coalition groups and the members of the country involved in the fight against terrorism. This not only protects their lands but protects other places in the world.

Nonparticipating countries must not wait until terrorism is embedded in their country. They must act before terrorism spreads into their boundaries and their country. It is hard to destroy terrorist groups once they embed themselves into a country. The terrorist groups destroy the government's ability to defend its citizens, and in most cases the citizens of their country will migrate to other parts of the world because it's not safe for them.

Coalition groups who join the fight against terrorism in countries occupied by terrorist groups will be a deterrent to suicide bombers, women sex slaves, childhood soldiers and destruction of the country's culture.

There is hope that when coalition groups join the fight against terrorism everywhere, the world will have some stability in the Middle Eastern world. It is my sincere desire that when coalition groups join the fight against terrorism, the Islamic State will be defeated and the country will find some kind of stability and there will be the ability to function on their own, in time, without the aid of other countries. The coalition groups that join the fight against terrorism, not only will bring peace and stability to the country which they defend; but also bring peace and stability to the country where they are citizens.

Chapter 8

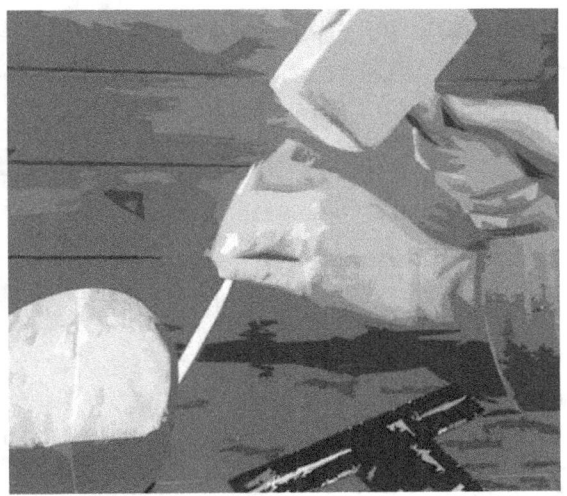

Rebuilding a Country After Occupation of a Terrorist Organization

When a country has been occupied by a terrorist group such as ISIS, the task of rebuilding is a major operation. Countries should be willing to come together and furnish aid and help rebuild Syria and Iraq. As countries in the world detach themselves from the rebuilding of a country during the removal of a terrorist group, it will delay the recovery of a country which has been occupied by terrorist groups. It is the duty of all peace-loving countries to furnish aid and building materials. Other forms of aid can be provided such as engineering or medical personnel. It is essential that a country that has been occupied by a terrorist group rebuild their hospitals and medical facilities. They need to have training for medical personnel to enable a country to take care of its medical needs. Education in the fields of medical technology, to help take care of patients, is needed. This country needs the advanced medical equipment to be able to treat the patients that are suffering from the stress of war and disease and injuries that are caused by the terrorist groups such as ISIS.

The need for global aid is highly essential, especially pharmaceutical supplies, and the men and women that are trained in dispensing much needed medications. It is important for the scientist to produce their own medications. They must produce all kinds of pharmaceuticals in the medical field in an occupied country. The country needs to open its lines of communication with other countries for many of these medical needs. This not only stimulates economic growth, it also produces revenues for the country supplying the pharmaceutical supplies.

It is essential that law enforcement agencies and the operation of a newly formed government be put in place as quickly as possible so that the country can begin to function without the aid of other countries. The law enforcement agencies in the newly formed government must be a part of the newly formed government's military community. The newly formed government must have a strong military presence. The law enforcement agencies and the military department of government should be a strong protection force for the citizens of the country. The new government should respect the rights of its citizens as far as freedom to worship, freedom to choose the leaders of their country and freedom to express their thoughts without fear of repression or threats on their lives. The newly formed government must have a free election system to enable its citizens to vote and have a say-so in operations of their government and laws in their country.

The farmers and other food producers in the country must be put in place immediately so that the country can begin producing food supplies. It would be of great value to open a country to export and import to other countries to strengthen the economy of the new government.

Technical support will be needed to help the country rebuild their homes and their infrastructures. Experts in the following fields are crucial in building a new government. Those in military science, education, in engineering, psychology and technology in all fields will be needed to rebuild a country when it has been devastated by the occupation of terrorist groups such ISIS.

A newly formed government must be a government that protects all of its citizens from mistreatments, especially women and people who have been devastated by the terrorist activity. A new government must be able to stop greed and crime and illegal operations such as the black market and the theft of government property and supplies before it takes place. This is done through law enforcement agencies and other agencies that are assigned to aid the operations of government. The country and the men and women who have been designated to take part in the government's operations, have to take charge. New governments must put in place laws and regulations that will keep hate groups and terrorist groups from operating within its borders.

When a terrorist group organization is captured or found kidnapping people within a country, they should have swift punishment applied to them. In the newly formed government, there should be strict laws and regulations concerning the recruiting and training of childhood soldiers.

Newly formed governments should have strict rules and regulations when it comes to hiring and paying people wages for their jobs and their job performance. They should have fair wages for the work that they produce for the employer. The civil right of all citizens in the formed country must and should be protected by the government. It should be the government's agenda to not allow any threats, destruction or the killing of innocent people.

We know that the terrorist group ISIS will be difficult to defeat because of the presence of other countries that support them. There is hope. There is enough hope in the world that will make it possible for Syria and Iraq to overcome the obstacles that non-coalition countries may cause.

The person within you is alive in the minds and the hearts of the people who have gone into refugee camps and migrated to other countries. It is the desire of all peace-loving people around the world that when the country which they migrate from becomes stable and they can live in their country without fear of suicide bombers, kidnapping, destruction of their property and the killing of their families will cease, I'm confident that some of these people will return and help rebuild their country.

I believe that when you read this book, you will find some way to help stop the dangerous course that terrorist groups have made.

The aid that you give to help rebuild countries such as Syria and Iraq, will protect the people in that country and give them a new sense of hope and a safe place to live. They will be able to control their own destiny when it comes to raising their family, when it comes to social events, when it comes to participation in their government. They will be able to worship in the desired way of their religious beliefs as long as it doesn't dominate the religious rights of other people. To be able to do the same, all people will enjoy the God-given life that they have which no one has the right to destroy through evil means.

When you give aid to a country that has had any type of destruction caused by man or by nature or any other disaster, you encourage help from other countries in a disaster or a fight against terrorism.

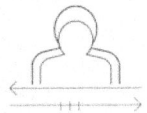

Chapter 9

Groups Through Foreign Aid and Assistance from Around the World

Helping rebuild a country after it has been occupied by a terrorist organization not only helps the people, it will someday help protect other countries from terrorist organizations such as ISIS. It is essential that countries help a country that has been occupied by terrorists. Allies can help rebuild by donating materials, finances and other means of support for rebuilding a government. It is the duty of all peace-loving countries to come together and render whatever means of support needed to the destruction in a country that has been devastated by terrorist group leaders.

There are things that you can do to help a country that has been devastated. Small things such as donating clothing, donating building materials, donating farm equipment, and donating equipment that is essential to building a country so that they can function on their own.

In many cases countries have equipment and other tools that are essential to building a country that has been destabilized helping stable professionals such as mechanics to be able to rebuild equipment that has been left behind by the terrorist groups. We need to have Syria, Iraq and other Middle Eastern countries able to rid themselves of terrorist groups so countries can function without terrorist groups interfering with the government operations. When countries like Syria and Iraq are receiving aid from other countries, it weakens the contributing country's financial stability and makes it difficult for them to take care of their own people. This is why it is essential that peace-loving countries world wide all participate in aiding and rebuilding countries such as Syria, Iraq and Middle Eastern countries that have been devastated by the actions of terrorism.

I am sure that more peace-loving countries will join the coalition and will contribute finances and much needed supplies to enable newly formed governments in these countries to be able to survive on their own.

When countries contribute finances and much needed supplies to any disaster, man made or by terrorist groups, it will be a help in stabilizing world conditions. Who knows, the country that you help to become stabilized may some day help your country in a disaster of some kind. This includes the United States. America has stepped up to the plate in helping disasters in Iraq and Syria and other countries. The United States will overcome the terrorist recruiters and the hate groups that are operating in our borders through education, through technology and Psychologic Study that is available in our country.

Chapter 10

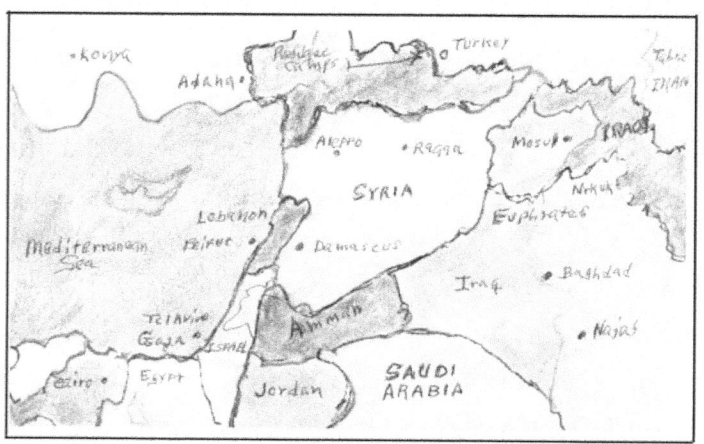

A Superpower Joins the Fight against Terrorism in Syria, with its Own Agenda

Since Russia had joined the fight against terrorism in Syria it is not clear what their main agenda is.

The United States and its collation member must be diplomatic when working with the Russian government. The fight against terrorism has taken a difficult role since the Russian military actions have taken place in Syria.

The United States and its collation members are not working together to destroy ISIS who are using Syria as a base camp to continue the fight in the Middle East.

Russia should be a part of the United States and its collation members who are fighting terrorism in the Middle East.

The Russian President and the President of Syria have their own agenda. At some point and time all the countries that are fighting in Syria must come together and find a diplomatic solution to the problem in Syria. Too many lives have been lost in Syria, because of the President of Syria and ISIS.

The outcome of the war in Syria should be to destroy ISIS and bring the Civil War to an end in a diplomatic manner, and have Russia withdraw its military presence from Syria. The Syrian government and its President should work out some kind of agreement and stop the killing of their own people.

If this is not done the Rebel forces are in great danger in Syria. The Syrian Rebels cannot stand against the Russian military power. The UN and countries around the world—most intervene in Syria to stop the blood-shed, shooting and stabbing in this country.

To stabilize Syria will be good for all countries around the world. Syria and Russia are one of the dominate forces in Syria at this time. The leader of Russian government, and the leader of Syria, Assad, both are birds of the same feather and they have the appetite for aggressiveness. What is troublesome about Putin is his aggressiveness. It is clear that Assad is in danger of losing his power in Syria and Russia is there to make sure he maintains his lordship in Syria.

The only way Syria will ever be stable is if Assad would step down. This country needs new leadership in its government. I do not see Assad stepping down, this is why Russia is in this country. Assad was losing to the rebels in his country. Assad and Putin are a bad combination for Syria. If Assad continues to control the government of Syria, there will continue to be chaos and confusing actions in Syria.

It is clear that Putin's plan is to destroy ISIS and the Rebels that are fighting the government of Assad.

The US and its counterparts must not let the men and women that are fighting the government of Assad fall into the hands of Assad's government. If this happens it would cause more bloodshed in Syria. It remains to be seen what will happen in Syria when ISIS is defeated in Syria. It will be hard for Syria to rebuild because a large part of the countries of the world do not like Assad and Putin's leadership. When ISIS is defeated in Syria the leaders of ISIS will find a new country to continue on its path of death and destruction. The only way to destroy ISIS is to destroy its leadership.

The UN and all nations of the world should get involved in the crises in the Middle East and Syria. When Russia entered the fight in Syria, a whole new possibility of new dangerous threats came about. This was created by a Russian presence in Syria.

When a civil war is going on, other countries should not get involved. When another country gets involved in a civil war the outcome will not be good. If a country gets involved in a civil war, it must be very diplomatic in its actions. Before a country gets involved in a conflict, it should search for a diplomatic end to the conflict. This could save lives and destruction that might come about.

When a country joins the UN, it should be heard, when its presence, its input, and a conflict comes about–such as what is happening in Syria today. The United States, Russia and other countries around the world should have one common goal: to stop the bloodshed in the Middle East.

When the Middle East becomes stable it will make all countries around the world a safer place in which to live. America and countries around the world are living under the threat of terrorism. Countries around the world must arm themselves and stop the terrorism groups with all means possible.

Syria and Iraq must be made stable by the countries in the Middle East themselves by the help of the UN and countries around the world who wish to make the world a safer place to live.

Because of the terror group in the Middle East people feel unsafe in their own countries. This is why countries must come together and find a solution to this problem.

Russia and a few other countries don't have agendas in that country to the thought of saving human lives. They just know that they want power to continue and to destroy that which is not theirs.

I do believe that at some point in time the Person Within You will give the minds of men and women the will and power to fight for humanity around the world.

The world must not give up the fight against hate groups and terrorism, because of Russia and other dictators in the world. The dictators will have his/her time at the table of justice. We must remember somehow and some time the good will win over the bad.

When things seem grim, hope is always near. The Person Within You would want you and the world to never stop fighting for peace and human rights.

In the world today all countries must maintain a strong army for their own safety. All countries around the world must display a peaceful agenda.

All countries must display diplomacy and be ready to defend themselves against the danger of a dictator, aggressor and terror groups, such as ISIS.

In most cases people will come together when it comes to keeping their country safe for them to live in. They will be willing to help build the military defense for their country. This will only come about if the government and leaders of the country display fair advice for all its citizens.

When a country has a strong military force it gives jobs and provides a steady tax income to that country. Military training is a good source of training for most young men and women. It would be good for the country if the younger generations could enter into the armed forces for a small period of time.

The aggressor will think twice before he attacks a country with a well-trained army.

When a country joins another that has a strong military power, the same as it, victory against the aggressor will come about. When a country joins the fight against the enemy of humanity it must have a true agenda not its own hidden agenda.

The United States and its counter parts must have a plan for the men and women who are fighting against the Syrian army, who is backed up by Russian military power. I fear that there will be great blood-shed if the rebels fall to the Syrian government.

I am sure some kind of solution can be made before it's too late for the men and women who are fighting against the Syrian army. If they were fighting the Syrian army only they would have a chance to win. Now that the Russians are back, the Syrian army will not win.

We can only fight ISIS and see what the outcome will be as long as the Russian military powers are in action in Syria.

We must not give up the fight against terrorism in the Middle Eastern countries. Where there is a will there is hope.

All the countries around the world must join in the fight for human rights and safety. This will happen and I hope it will be soon.

This is what the Person Within You is about; it's about the love for human kind.

Part II

Conclusion

Terrorism is very dangerous to all people in the world. There is no terrorist power that cannot be overcome. The desire and the will to fight terrorism wherever it might exist, will bring stability and stop the meaningless destruction and killings of innocent people in the world.

We know that through the will of peace-loving people and humanitarians, the world will overcome the terrorist acts from roots of terrorists such as ISIS and other terrorist organizations. It is my desire that countries around the world that believe in justice and humanity will come together and defeat the terrorist group organizations that are causing destruction and death. Through coalition groups that are fighting terrorism today and more peace-loving countries joining these coalitions, the war against terrorism will subside.

Not only do coalition groups help protect the countries that are battling terrorism, it protects all peace-loving countries in the world who do not want terrorism to be operating in their country. Terrorism and hate groups in countries interrupts the normal functions of families and operations of government in which that group occupies. All hate groups, and terrorist organizations have one thing in common, and that is to threaten, to destroy, to kill and cause destruction in the country that they are in. People of all races, all religious beliefs and all functions of life should be free of the interruptions of hate groups and terrorist groups who may cause them to fear for their lives in their own country and when they travel to other countries around the world.

We must remember that to maintain safety and stability and be free to enjoy social events and other activities in our lives, we must all join the fight against terrorism in any way that we can. When people in America and people around the world can join the fight against terrorism, it will make it safe in America and all countries. We will and we must overcome hate groups and terrorism of all kinds. The will to overcome terrorist organizations and other hate groups will bring victory to America and its allies and save thousands of lives. The elements of surprise are great strategies to use when fighting terrorism or any other type of warfare.

Comments From the Author

As a member of the human society, I would like to express my views when it comes to terrorism in the world today.

Terrorist groups are killing innocent people around the world. Terrorist groups are using threats of death and destruction in Syria and Iraq and other parts of the world.

It is becoming unsafe for people in countries around the world to enjoy things the society provides. Pleasure, recreation, worship and things that they enjoy in their communities are metropolitan areas and in their governments.

You cannot feel safe traveling today because of terrorist activities. People do not feel safe at major events because of terroristic activities, and in some countries, including America, it is not safe to attend some sports events where large crowds of people are gathered.

It is my sincere desire to see the day again when traveling, attending sports events, just visiting a cafe or enjoying an outing is done without the fear of terrorist bombings or threats.

All hate groups and terrorist groups have things in common. They can kill you in your church, your movie theaters, your schools, your sports events and they have no regard for human life or the rights of people to live without fear of death and destruction.

I truly believe that together as human beings we can defeat these terroristic atrocities by fighting with all the resources that are available to us, against terrorism.

The book "The Person Within You" was written to give the reader an idea of how dangerous terrorism is around the world and how it could affect all people. Terror groups are a threat to you in your own community and in your own home.

ISIS is one of the world's dangerous terrorist groups. They will kill your young men and your young women. They recruit them to kill innocent people. If you are recruited by ISIS or any other terrorist group, they will not tell you that you will be a candidate for suicide bombings. They will not tell you that they will kill you before they allow you leave their organization.

The book "The Person Within You" will give the reader some idea of ISIS' recruiting methods. We see ISIS fighting in Syria and Iraq. ISIS does not plan to stop its threats in these countries. Their plan is to spread terrorism world wide. "The Person Within You" will tell you that ISIS is not invisible. Together we can defeat them with coalitions forces in the International Community. ISIS can be defeated. If America and its allies around the world accomplish it, ISIS and its terrorist group counterparts can be eliminated. I am confident that all nations that have love for humanity and wish to protect their heritage, their museums, their historical history and their religious beliefs, can come together and defeat terrorist groups and their dictators.

It is my desire that the book "The Person Within You" will be a tool to fight terrorism. I hope that after you read this book, it will help you to fight for the love of humanitarianism. The examples of what you can do to fight against terrorism are:

1. Support your neighborhood law enforcement agent.
2. Support your Christian organizations.
3. Support the Islamic groups that are fighting against ISIS.

When all these factors that have been mentioned about safety and how to defeat the terrorist group organizations are put in place, I'm sure we will see a decrease in the destruction of countries, the killing and threats of innocent people that are impacted by terrorism. After this factor they will be able to function in a normal manner.

I acknowledge the brave news reporters and media people who have given us a first-hand account of these events the terrorist groups are responsible for. The news media men and women who have given their lives in Syria and Iraq while reporting the news should be remembered. The Japanese reporter and U.S. reporter who were beheaded in a televised public execution by the Islamic state must be remembered and honored for losing their lives.

I continue to give thanks to the news media and the brave reporters who are risking their lives to give us a first-hand look at terrorism throughout the world and its effects on every culture.

The element of surprise can help you defeat your enemy.

Glossary:

A

Armed Forces: the combined military, naval and air forces of the nation.
Action: operation
Associate: one that companies another
Artifact: any object remaining from another time or culture
Agenda: a list of things to be done: program
Affiliate: to be united in a relationship
Assessments: the act of attributing

B

Blood-shed: taking of life
Bomber: one that bombs

C

Cooperation: working together
Community: an organized body
Charge: charging someone with a misdeed
Communication: allowing exchange of ideas or messages

Candidate: a person who seeks a job or position
Captured: to capture after a struggle
Coalition: an association of nations for a common cause

D

Divine: a person ordained or service in a Christian church
Destroy: to cause the death of someone
Displayed: to make visible, to bring to view
Detected: to uncover
Destroying: to cause complete ruin
Disguising: to hide or conceal
Dangerous: unsafe

E

Extremist: one who holds extreme views
Enforcement: to enforce the low
Eliminating: to get rid of, by banishment or execution
Engineering: the practical applications of scientific and mathematical principles.

F

Foreign aid: given aid to a foreign country
Freedom: the state of not being in confinement or servitude

G

Grave: having great consequence or weight

H

Hate: extreme hostility and dislike
Humanity: the human race
Humanitarians: concerned with human welfare and the alleviation of suffering
Historical: history based on people or events of the past

I

Islamic: adj: Muslims lands in which they predominate
Innocent: free from evil and corruption
Investigation: careful search or systematic inquiry
Information: something told or facts learned
Infrastructures: basic installations and facilities

J

Judicial: the judges, courts or their functions

K

Knowledge: that which is known

L

Leader: one who is highest in rank or authority

M

Museum: a place for persevering and exhibiting historical objects
Mistreatment: to treat wrongly or badly
Military: the armed forces

N

Neighborhood: a particular community
Nonparticipating: not getting involved

O

Organization: a group of people united in a relationship having some interest
Operations: the act of putting into function

P

Problems: a situation that presents difficulty
Psychology: the thought processes characteristics of an individual
Propaganda: any widespread promotion of particular ideas

R

Ruthlessness: without pity or compassion
Refugees: one who flees home or country
Representative: one who are authorized to act of others
Recruiter: one who seeks new members
Religious: concerned with God and beliefs

S

Sympathizers: one that acts or reacts in sympathy of another
Synagogues: house of worship of a Jewish congregation

Suspected: to be guilty without proof
Stability: the strength to stand or endure

T

Terrorism: the use of force of threats to intimidate
Technical: dealing with applied sciences
Technology: the science of the practical or industrial arts

U

Understanding: the faculty of thinking

V

Vulnerable: Open to attack and capture

W

Within: inside the limits

Proceeds From
The Book

A portion of the proceeds from the sale of the book The Person Within You has been dedicated to helping refugees and migration victims who have been devastated by terrorism in Syria, Iraq and the Middle East countries

Author's Artwork

The face of Terrorism

Author's Artwork

Blood-shed A.D.

Author's Artwork

Death caused by Terrorism

Author's Artwork

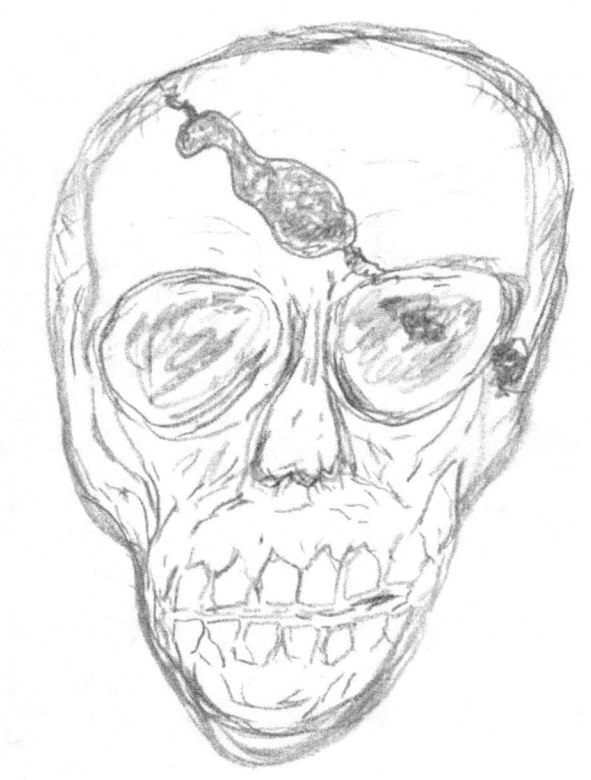

Death caused by gun shot to the skull

Author's Artwork

You have the right to worship,
as long as it does not
endanger other humankind

Author's Artwork

The untruth of terrorism

Death by

World terrorism

Author's Artwork

A child training to become a
suicide bomber

Author's Artwork

Semblance of victims killed by
terrorism, world wide

Author's Artwork

Countries free of terrorism

Author's Artwork

A country devastated
by terrorism

References

1. "It Is About Islam" by Glenn Becker

2. "The Psychopathology of Everyday Life" by Sigmund Freud, p. 72

3. "Rise of ISIS" by J. Sekulow, p. 92

4. "The Psychology of Terror" edited by Chris E. Stout, p. 4, 21

If you were inspired from reading

The Person Within You

Please share with us, how you will fight terrorism.

Please leave a review on Amazon.com

Also available in Kindle

Order Form
$12.95/book
+ $3.50 s & h

Name: _____

Address:_____

_____

Credit Card type: _____

CC #: _____

exp: _____   Security code: _____

Number of books _____

Please send order form to
BTBI c/o Justice the Salute
17011 Lincoln Ave #408
Parker, CO 80134